BLACK AND WHITE

BRIGID BROPHY

BLACK AND WHITE

A PORTRAIT OF
AUBREY BEARDSLEY

STEIN AND DAY / *Publishers* / New York

First published in the United States of America by
Stein and Day/*Publishers*, 1969

First published in Great Britain by
Jonathan Cape Ltd, 1968
Copyright © 1968 by Brigid Brophy

Library of Congress Catalog Card No. 69-15906

An abbreviated version of this essay first
appeared in the *Atlantic Monthly*

The author is grateful to all owners
who have kindly given permission to
reproduce works in their possession.

Printed in Great Britain
Stein and Day/*Publishers*/7 East 48 Street, New York, N.Y. 10017

LIST OF ILLUSTRATIONS

LIVE (love) now: die sooner or later.

That, classically, is the purport of lyrical art. Aubrey Beardsley was above all a lyrical artist – but one who was pounded and buckled into an ironist by the pressure of knowing, which he did virtually from the outset, that for him death would be not later but sooner.

In his terrible, biological haste, he was first an infant prodigy and then a prodigious worker – though, in a delicate social gesture that would suit one of his masked pierrots, he disguised his hard work in evening dress and sophistication. He died of consumption in 1898, when he was twenty-five. He must be – as well as, simply, a very great artist – the most intensely and electrically erotic artist in the world. But he is an erotic artist for whom Cupid himself can prefigure death. In one (1) of the decorations Beardsley drew to his own sinister 'Ballad of a Barber', a sonsy, callipygian, wing-flirting amoretto comes flouncing along in profile silhouette, like a boy tart on the beat. This beat, however, is also a march to the scaffold and a road to Calvary. Beardsley's Cupid is shouldering not quiver and arrows but gallows and noose.

Beardsley is lyrical by virtue of his gift of line, which re-sembles the gift of melodic invention. Sheerly, Beardsley's lines, like great tunes, go up and down in beautiful places. It is true that they often, by the same stroke, represent objects: but never for purposes of reportage or narrative. Not a dot is put in for description's sake. Beardsley inserts nothing on the grounds that it was or would be there. He attends only to what, by compulsion of the design, should be there.

Illustrator though he was by choice, and sometimes of his own literary fictions, and though he was also (which not all writers are) a devouring reader, Beardsley the draughtsman isn't in the least 'literary'. The tension that dominates all his compositions is entirely in the design and the medium. None of it is borrowed from the incidents, and still less the characters, of any story he may adopt. This makes it less strange than it superficially looks, in a personality so passionately literate, that Beardsley *didn't*, after the Hamlet picture of his teens, much draw on or from Shakespeare. (Dickens, whom Beardsley as a schoolboy accurately diagnosed as a cockney Shakespeare, he stopped quarrying after he had, at the age of eleven, decorated a set of place mats with Dickensian characters.) Shakespeare was *too* literary for Beardsley's requirements; the images too perfectly fused into their literary vehicles of character and action. Beardsley could make more of the literature *in* the music of Wagner.

What Beardsley plunders from literature are matters common to all the arts: pure style, pure image. Pope figures to him as the epitome of the rococo, Ben Jonson of the baroque. (In this sense, Shakespeare *has* no style.) Out of the given style Beardsley sets his virtuoso line to pluck a pure, self-sufficient image. His sequences of drawings establish series of related images or conduct a single image through metamorphic variations. A Beardsley

sequence is like a sonnet sequence. Yet it is never the literary content of an image that concerns him. His portraits, including those of himself, are less portraits than icons. He is drawing not persons but personages; he is dramatizing not the relationships between personalities but the pure, geometric essence of relationship. He is out to capture sheer tension: tension contained within, and summed up by, his always ambivalent images.

Sometimes the image is presented, in its complete irony and ambiguity, through a single piercing contrast – a solo black outline that severs a white area into two spaces. The second (2) of the two drawings Beardsley made, for his Juvenal illustrations, of Bathyllus (the pantomimist whom Maecenas had a crush on, according to Tacitus[1]) lies as firm, fine and inscrutable in its white oblong as a Greek vase-painting on its ground. Indeed, Beardsley has borrowed from the vase-painters' technique – and from their subjects' physique: in both cases, to satiric purpose. The implicit homosexuality of Greek boxers and athletes Beardsley has expanded into the explicit gesture of an invitation to buggery; and the over-muscled heroic Greek body he has bloated out into Roman blowsiness. The flabby femaleness of Bathyllus's flesh Beardsley decorates by comically flinging over his shoulder something remarkably like a Wagnerian maiden's plait – which is yet

[1] *Annals*, I, 54. Beardsley was illustrating the very brief mention, in Juvenal's Sixth Satire, of 'the effeminate Bathyllus ... acting Leda in the ballet'. (Brodie's translation.)

BATHYLLVS

also a displaced horse's tail: the very blatancy with which
Bathyllus prances with monumentally spread buttocks
turns on the ironic joke that his pose is one which, in
equestrian monuments, is conventionally noble. The
metamorphic suggestion that Bathyllus is animal from
the waist down renders him on the instant a monster.
That he is a monster simultaneously attractive and re-
pulsive (people who are blatantly sexually available are
available to *us* but not *exclusively* to us, so that they pro-
voke jealousy simultaneously with desire) is incarnated,
by the most economic of means, in the brilliant *contrap-
posto* between his lewd, inviting left hand and his crude,
sign-posting right (which indicates so plainly what the
horse's tail has been displaced in favour of); and this contra-
position is in turn made meaningful by the simple, masterly
intellectual *rightness* of the figure's placing in its space,
whose organic importance to the composition Beardsley
has emphasized by framing it in a double line.

The economy of the Bathyllus drawing is the opposite
of impoverished: the rich imaginative material is all con-
densed into the single outline. By the converse process,
Beardsley could tease material out from the image and
spin it into a decorative setting which, because its metaphors repeat those of the image itself, intensifies the image
it enshrines. Beardsley's conversion to Catholicism, which
his recent commentators rightly do not take very seriously
as a religious act, was a logical continuation of his work.
The contemplation – the cult – of an image is the essence
of Beardsley's art. His elaborate decorative schemes are

(3)

jewelled monstrances for the display of highly ambivalent hosts or altars enshrining relics of dangerously numinous, monstrous saints: never more so than in the two great pictures, 'The Baron's Prayer' (3), from his Pope sequence, and 'Volpone Adoring His Treasure' (4), which actually and expressly depict metaphors of their own essence by ironically depicting acts of warped worship at satirized altars.

It is again an altar – flattened, diagrammatized, seen in plan – that Beardsley creates, in one of the most lethally ambivalent of all his images, for his front cover to *The Rape of the Lock* (5). In an oval that suggests a miniature painting hung on a drawing-room wall and thereby betokens Pope's miniature and domesticated epic, Beardsley places 'the fatal engine', the scissors, reaching murderously up towards that lock of curly hair which, as Pope quite consciously intended ('Oh hadst thou, cruel! been content to seize/Hairs less in sight, or any hairs but these!'), stands symbolic substitute for pubic hair. At the same time, the oval is the mirror on Belinda's dressing-table. The glass stares direct at the artist, at Beardsley; and what he shews reflected in it is his own castration complex. At this altar, he is the sacrificed victim, doomed to sexual frustration and death. The lock of hair makes allusion to the cutting of a few symbolic hairs from the head of the animal victim in classical sacrifices; and by the disposition of the lock and the scissors Beardsley sketches a far-removed memory of the skull-mask of classical altars and funerary sculpture.

18

VOLPONE

Simultaneously, this stunningly elegant design makes a metaphor of the ambiguity of elegance itself, through the tension it sets up between its elements: on the one hand, the budding, twirling rococo candlesticks (in whose flame the sacrificial hair is by implication to be burnt), plus their silhouetted echo in the sides of the frame – which consists at once of a pair of further candlesticks and of bulbously buttocked female torsos; and, on the other, those inexorable straight, ruled, reduplicated black lines, which visibly act out the shearing and severing deed of the scissors. Beardsley's elegance is budding, rotund, fruitful – but also disdainful and severe; he is an artist who will soon be compelled to the ultimate act of good taste, that of leaving living to be done by the servants.

Inevitably Beardsley's own regular method of work was by the artificial light from two candlesticks. His worktable was a sacrificial altar. All his designs were images whose very working was an act of desperate invocation.

Destined to cult, he was destined pre-eminently to the Catholic cult of the Madonna. In Beardsley's life, his mother is as regularly there, and his father as regularly absent or unnoticeable, as the Madonna and Saint Joseph in Christian iconography. His elder sister, Mabel (I wonder if Wilde named Mabel Chiltern for her?), figured to Beardsley as the mother writ one size smaller. Mabel takes several, and seldom un-erotic, rôles in his œuvre: the Madonna writ, so to speak, as Mary Magdalen. Socially, Beardsley was dependent on his mother and sister to hostess

for him. As a child, he probably felt an unusual material dependence on his mother, since, unusually for the period, she, as well as the father, worked. And as a dying man Beardsley returned to the child's state of bodily dependence on his mother. In Beardsley's novel, after Venus and Tannhäuser have made love, Venus is literally carried – 'in a nice, motherly way' – to bed in the arms of her 'manicure', Mrs Marsuple, who ends the chapter with a speech that must have often been made to the young Mabel and Aubrey Beardsley (who were perhaps in some sense lovers, too): 'Come along, children … it's time you were both in bed.'

Beardsley, who drew a boyish 'Hail Mary' long before he turned Catholic, made the Madonna and Child the subject of one of his least Beardsleyesque adult exercises, the 'large Christmas card' distributed with No. 1 of the *Savoy*. But it is in ways less direct and more sardonic that he most characteristically treats the pair – that pair in which the child is doomed in advance to pre-decease his mother, and, though he is as instinct with godhead as Beardsley was precociously bursting with genius, is ritually stuck in perpetual infancy, for ever needing the protection of his mother's arms. A small statuette of the Madonna and Child, jewelled and lacy in the Spanish taste, presides over Beardsley's full-scale illustration (6) to his Barber ballad. (The ballad's story is, surely, extrapolated from *The Rape of the Lock*, which Beardsley illustrated in the same year, 1896. Beardsley recounts explicitly the erotically murderous wish symbolized in the Baron's seemingly un-

AUBREY BEARDSLEY.

(6)

serious assault on Belinda.) The grouping of the tiny, crowned cult-figures is repeated by the pair in front, to ironic point: the Madonna protects the child in her care, but Beardsley's Barber is about to kill the adolescent princess entrusted to his.

In the same year Beardsley carried the image of the mother-and-child group to its utmost sardonic and high-comedic pitch. In 'The Ascension of Saint Rose of Lima' (7), the child, though grown-up, is still enfolded within the outline of the protector's mantle, and is, as in the Barber drawing, female. So, it should be supererogatory to say, is the Madonna. It is by a singular infelicity, of the kind ironic artists seem fated to in their interpreters, that a recent study of Beardsley's eroticism mistakes the erotic point of the drawing by supposing the saint to be ascending 'in the embrace of the heavenly bridegroom'. Not she. As a matter of fact, the Madonna is saving her from an earthly bridegroom. The very pretty, camp and Firbankian passage in Beardsley's novel *Under The Hill* which this drawing illustrates recounts how, on the morning of her wedding day, Saint Rose 'perfumed herself and painted her lips, and put on her wedding frock, and decked her hair with roses' and then, from a hill outside Lima, spent 'some moments calling tenderly upon Our Lady's name'. In answer the Madonna descends, kisses her and carries her up to heaven.

In 'The Ascension', the Spanish-style laciness of the statuette in the Barber picture has turned Peruvian; it has all slipped to and concentrated itself on the underskirt of

the saint's 'wedding frock', disclosed by the catching-up of her garment by that punning and now pinning bridal rose fallen from her hair. (Another has drifted further yet on the mystical slipstream and alighted to play peacock's eye in the tail of the Madonna's robe.) Perhaps Beardsley had in mind his sister, whose conversion to Catholicism preceded his own, as he laid the saint's breast against the Madonna's and her cheek against the Madonna's face, and then delicately closed the saint's eyes in the bliss of gratified lesbianism. (I can find no evidence they so much as met; but if poetic justice exists, surely Mabel Beardsley had a love affair with Heather Firbank.) It is Saint Rose (a thoroughly baroque saint, canonized in 1671) and the Madonna who ascend – and Rubens, Murillo, the standard Counter-Reformation composition for Assumptions of the Virgin, the orgasmic smile on the face of Bernini's Saint Teresa, the entire baroque, the very concept of saintly ecstasy and, indeed, Catholicism itself that are sent up.

Even when she is not present and personified, the mother dictates Beardsley's very point of view. Beardsley was a latter-day Mannerist. The common complaint[1] of his contemporaries against his figures, especially his women, was the complaint made at all periods against all mannered figures, that they are too tall and have necks like giraffes. His lovely, gentle and unsentimental drawing (8) (once

[1]Cf. Weintraub, VI and Appendix.

26

(8)

owned by Oscar Wilde[1]) of Mrs Patrick Campbell was said to make her 'nine feet high'. Mannerism: mama-ism. The elegance of these elongated persons, who are so au fait in the world, is a memory of adults, and quintessentially the mother, seen in child's-eye-view; the slight melancholy they so exquisitely wear is draped on them by the child's sense of their high inaccessibility.

Mannerism is in itself a style that murmurs of perversity, its elongations a visual drawl that mimics sexual languor. It shews a child's-eye-view, but the child is precocious. Beardsley, who *was* a precocious child, remained one – as Oscar Wilde[2] pointed out. It is the characteristic of precocious children that, in childhood, they are astonishing because they resemble adults. In adulthood, they are often – like Mozart and Beardsley – astonishing because they resemble children. The genius of Beardsley's eroticism is precisely the quality Freud ascribed to the sexuality of children: polymorphous perversity.

It is only the most obvious manifestation of this quality that Beardsley's subject-matter, by his own choice, encompasses virtually the whole sexual spectrum, from delicate bestiality (Venus, in his novel, masturbates her pet unicorn, Adolphe, every morning before breakfast)

[1] who wrote to her in February 1894 (when she was playing in the second London run of Pinero's *The Second Mrs Tanqueray*) asking to present Beardsley to her. She gave Beardsley a sitting (see V. & A. exhibition catalogue, no. 481) and Beardsley's drawing of her was published in the first *Yellow Book*.

[2] Quoted by Weintraub (IV): Beardsley's *Salome* drawings 'are like the naughty scribbles a precocious boy makes on the margins of his copybooks'.

AUBREY
BEARDSLEY.

(9)

(11)

to flagellation – which he depicts in the beautiful 'Earl Lavender' illustration (9) that seems to capture even the slight social embarrassment that must accompany actually getting down to an evening's whipping.

Whether Beardsley himself ever actually got down to incest with Mabel is a question almost beside the point. In imagination he certainly was incestuous: he was, in imagination, everything; and for him the imagination was everything. Although it was Tannhäuser he plundered from Wagner for his novel, it was very likely the brother-sister incest theme in *The Ring* that caused Beardsley to make a personal cult of (instead of just admiring, as he did Beethoven) Wagner. He recognized, moreover, the eroticism, the fetishism, in the general cult of Wagner by Wagnerites. His most successful transposition of Wagner's eroticism does not depict the Wagnerian personages at all, but simply the sensuality with which the audience listens to *Tristan und Isolde*. In 'The Wagnerites' (10), it is the audience (all, with one, no doubt homosexual exception, women) who are collectively Isolde; and they are an Isolde who is *gulping* the love potion. No more is it relevant whether Beardsley was, as he hinted to several friends, who didn't always believe him, homosexual. Beardsley kept a foot in either camp – a foot wearing, moreover, a kinky boot, no doubt of the pattern he drew on the feet of the hero (11) of his novel.

Beardsley's perversity goes well beyond his signing his work with an emblem said to be (in, presumably, the anthropological sense) a fetish symbolizing sexual inter-

MESSALINA.

C

ET IN ARCADIA
EGO

THE SAVOY

AN ILLUSTRATED QUARTERLY

No. 2   April 1896   Price **2/6** net

EDITED
BY

ARTHUR
SYMONS

AUBREY BEARDSLEY

course; and his polymorphism goes worlds beyond his alertness to the fetishist value (in the psychosexual sense) of hair (12) (and in the 'Lysistrata' series Beardsley can make intricate coiffures of even pubic hair), of tiny pointed shoes (13), and of hats. (Beardsley's 'Choosing the New Hat' (14) is so fetishist as almost to illustrate choosing a new fetish.) Rather, his imagination seems to be in at the actual infantile origin of fetishism. His vision is permanently that of a child lying in bed watching his mother dress for a dinner-party. His fantasy hangs this here, tries the effect of that there: everything is a jewel, and everything is a sexual organ. He is allured, yet afraid to touch: driven back on a cold minuteness of detailed attention, and yet passionately curious, with the emotional and involved curiosity children give to sex. The very fastidiousness of his line demonstrates the importance of touching and the fear that has to be overcome in order to do it.

Beardsley's imagination is for ever lying in bed dressing and re-dressing his mother – and doing it inappropriately. The child's protest against his inexperience, against the ban on touching, is to glory in his ignorance. He does not know which sexual organs are appropriate to which sex; he makes deliberate howlers in order to howl against his exclusion from adult knowledge. And even that bitter intellectual howl is a mask for a yet earlier cry of pure terror, the boy child's terror at the discovery that his mother does not possess the organ he so values as a pendant and ornament on his own body. They are all breasts and penises, these decorative motifs of Beardsley's, these

36

(15)

drooping swags of fruit, these swaying jewels and those swinging tassels – which already dandify a cane in one of the grotesques (15) for the *Bon-Mots* series[1]; and Beardsley hangs them in places so inappropriate, blatant or bizarre as to create an effect of perversity – or, indeed, of pure terror, as he does by that stroke of nightmare genius that makes him a fin-de-siècle Goya when, illustrating *The Murders in the Rue Morgue* (16), he dangles a disdainfully decorative chandelier ear-ring from the lobe of the slaughterous orang-outang.

It is his own polymorphism that animates the meta-morphism of Beardsley's images. His decorative forms are ambiguous in matter, caught in the act of changing from one substance into another; his human figures are am-biguous in sex. He will depict a hermaphrodite body direct, as he does in the *Salome* title page[2] or in his 'The Mirror of Love' (17) design: 'Whatever you may say', wrote the publisher who rejected it, 'the figure is her-maphrodite.'[3] Or he will clothe the figure and, in doing so, transvest it – and, by that token, invest it, as he does Mademoiselle de Maupin (18) or Mrs Pinchwife (19), with a charm as deeply defiant as Rosalind is of sex-classification. Are they female fops, these personages of Beardsley's: female dandies: female effeminates, even? Or are they male hoydens, male tomboys, boy butches?

[1]Weintraub (IV) reports Beardsley's apologizing for his pallor with the explanation that he had caught cold by accidentally leaving the tassel off his cane.
[2]Reproduced in Reade, *Beardsley*, plate 274.
[3]Quoted by Reade, *Beardsley*, note 386.

(16)

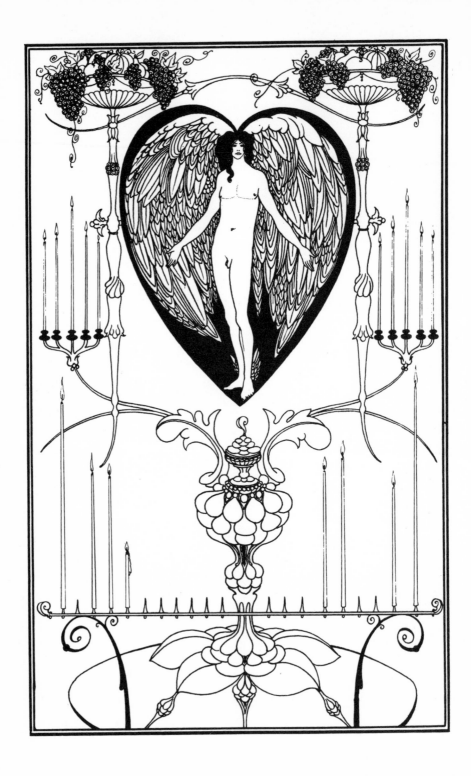

Alternatively, Beardsley translates the male/female mixture into a human/animal mixture. He does this to grotesque effect (the grotesquerie being borrowed from the dressed-up animals of circuses and organ-grinders) in his frontispiece to Juvenal,[1] where a sedan-chair is carried by monkeys in livery – a theme adumbrated earlier in a drawing (20) for the *Bon-Mots* series. Elsewhere Beardsley adopts a ready-made motif, like his favourite one of the satyr, and presses an ironic poetry from the fact that the male/female mixture created by infantile muddle and infantile fantasy has already been transformed by mythology into the nostalgic figure of a human/animal mixture belonging to a golden, partly heroic, partly alarming and wholly irrecoverable past.

Beardsley translates mythology back into the language of the unconscious, wherein the golden age equals childhood, by the very piquancy with which he disposes his satyr (21)[2] in the rôle of precocious child. In contrast to the well-dressed, well-mannered, civilized woman, the satyr is untamed, primitive. Yet he is older than the meadow he sits in. It is he, the primitive, who plays the tutor – and who has so much, of a so corrupting nature, to impart to his governess.

And, even so, a further metamorphosis is possible, for Beardsley, in the already human/animal mixture. The animal portion may be further transformed – into a thing.

[1]Reproduced in Reade, *Beardsley*, plate 371.
[2]This drawing, for the front cover of Volume V of the *Yellow Book*, was withdrawn by the publisher as a result of the Wilde scandal in 1895.

MRS PINCHWIFE

AB

(21)

The cloven-hoof feet of the leading fruit bearer (22) Beardsley depicted for his novel are almost the goat feet of rococo and Regency furniture. The creature is a walking, a stalking console table. For Beardsley it is not alone fountains, chairbacks, candle flames that are phallic. For him, as for Fuseli, it is human figures themselves (23). And one could say of many of Beardsley's landscapes (24) what Freud[1] said of 'many of the landscapes seen in dreams, especially those that contain bridges or wooded mountains', namely that they 'may be readily recognized as descriptions of the genitals'. The mountain where Beardsley's Venus keeps state, the hill of *Under The Hill*, is a pun on the *mons Veneris*. Effortlessly Beardsley composes in the symbolic idiom of the unconscious (which was not invented by Freud, as one of Beardsley's scholarly commentators seems to suppose when he declares Beardsley's painting of a woman contemplating a mouse (25) 'miraculous' on the grounds that 'Freud's mythology was unknown in England in 1894.' Heigh-ho: was it known in Greece when Sophocles wrote the *Oedipus Rex*?).

The polymorphism Beardsley preserved from infancy is not only mirrored directly in what he depicted. It is metaphored in the very eclecticism of his style – an eclecticism so fundamental to his personality that it extends even to an eclecticism among the arts: Beardsley was a musical prodigy, not only performing in semi-public but

[1] *The Interpretation of Dreams*, VI(E), translated by A. A. Brill.

D

performing his own compositions, even before he was a precocious draughtsman or writer.

The elasticity which Beardsley needed in order to exploit his temperamental eclecticism he acquired, I suspect, thanks to what looks like a childish method of work. The fastidiousness of his final drawings evidently represents a naive perfectionism; for as a rule it seems[1] to have been built up by an unfastidious process of pencil doodling and pencil sketching, over which, all on the same piece of cartridge paper, he imposed his final line by brush or nib.

Beardsley's novel underwent so many important changes, its title being at various times *Venus and Tannhäuser* and *Under The Hill* and its hero varying from Tannhäuser to the Abbé Aubrey to the Abbé Fanfreluche, that it looks as though Beardsley applied the same method to literature – and was, perhaps, to judge from his inability to finish his book, surprised that it was there less practical.

The method may even betoken another childish activity preserved. Going over the details of images to get them exactly correct is the imaginative technique of the masturbation-fantasist. When he portrayed himself (26) – not as a child but as an adult invalid – in the situation which gave his work its cardinal viewpoint, peeping out, dwarfed, from a vast tent of a bed, Beardsley hung his favourite tassels, perhaps as a mark that they were not for touching, *outside* the bed. One of his strangest and profoundest images (27), in manner anticipating a classical Braque, is

[1] Cf. Reade, *Beardsley*, p.22.

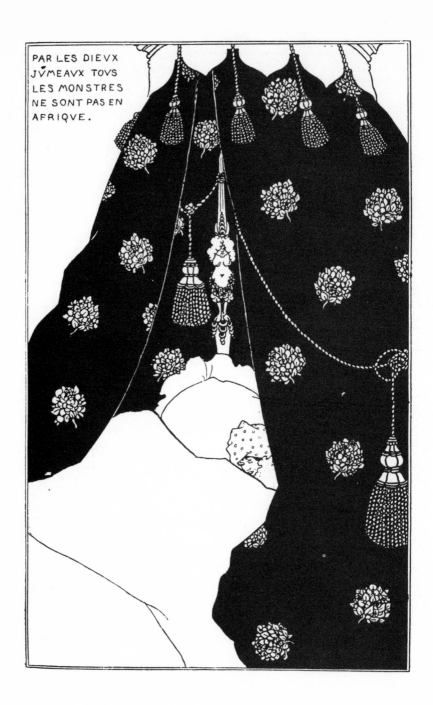

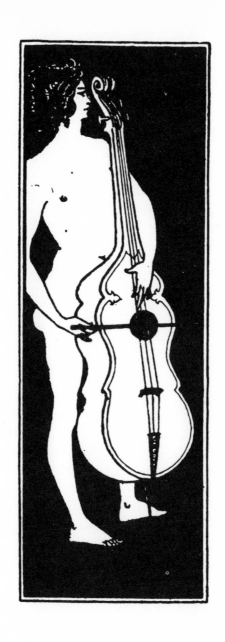

(27)

the naked double-bass player who is so obviously,[1] and with such musical calm, symbolically masturbating.

Only perhaps on such palimpsests, such scratch-pads, as he made of his drawings could Beardsley have so briefly accomplished his huge and daring revolution in his own (and presently the world's) taste. In the six years of his adult life, he evolved from self-imposed Burne-Jonesism and the medieval subject-matter imposed by his first major commission (to illustrate *Le Morte Darthur*) into high rococo and high baroque, virtually inventing a branch of *art nouveaux* as he went. (Even Walter Crane[2] could perceive, in 1911, that 'that strange decorative disease known as "L'Art Nouveau"', which some people considered a development of William Morris-ism, was 'really its antithesis'.) Now that Beardsley's revolution in taste has triumphed, it is hard – but necessary if one is to honour his courage – to remember how frowned on the eighteenth century was by the nineteenth. It must have seemed almost a perversity in itself that Beardsley should identify (28) his own loneliness with that of the clowns of his fellow-consumptive, Watteau, foretell his own death in terms of 'The Death of Pierrot' (29), and play on the fetishist and perverse motif of masks (whose carnival invitation to anonymous sexual encounter always hints at the statistical possibility of unknowingly committing incest) in the manner of Longhi. Even the sympathetic Robert Ross,

[1] Playing the violin had this significance for the child Freud mentions in *Totem and Taboo*, IV, 3.
[2] In *William Morris to Whistler*.

in his Beardsley memoir of 1908/9, remarked that 'Beardsley, many people think to the detriment of his style, turned his attention to the eighteenth century.'

Beardsley made the revolution deliberately and consciously. At the end of his life he was proposing, as the programme for a new magazine, 'that it should attack *untiringly & unflinchingly* the Burne-Jones & Morrisian medaeval [*sic*] business, & set up a wholesome 17th & 18th century standard of what picture-making should be'.[1] His own eclecticism and elasticity had not been wanton: he had worked a standard out of them. Perhaps Beardsley was able to pioneer the eighteenth-century revival by virtue of the happy chance of his being brought up in Brighton, that late and fine architectural monument of the eighteenth-century manner. Perhaps the high rococo-baroque mode Beardsley's eclecticism finally fixed on was the exotic late-rococo eclecticism of Brighton Pavilion itself, that ultimate Regency extravaganza which is also the first flicker of *art nouveau*.

Towards the end of his life, Beardsley could barely get through social intercourse without a haemorrhage. Whether or not he had ever been otherwise, the common speculation is surely correct that he was by then exiled from sexual intercourse. The giant erect phalluses of his 'Lysistrata' series (30) ache with sexual frustration. Beardsley, who once alluded to himself as a eunuch and could not have a tooth extracted without self-satirically

[1] Quoted by Weintraub, *Beardsley*, XI.

AUBREY BEARDSLEY

remarking on the phallic shape of what had been removed from him,[1] a point he had earlier made visually in one of the most literally bad-dream-like of his grotesques (31), a picture that might be captioned by Freud's statement 'The dream-work represents castration by ... the loss of teeth',[2] also illustrates Freud's dictum that the unconscious apprehends death as castration.[3] The castration-orgasm-death image of Salome kissing the Baptist's severed head, which is so merely silly in Wilde's text (*Salome* is the final proof that Wilde was a great comic writer, since it's comic unintentionally), is truly horrifying in Beardsley's drawing (32). Beardsley, so deeply prey to it himself, has incarnated in his drawing the aboriginal moment of infantile horror, the moment when the image of the mother is metamorphosed into the image of a castrator by virtue of the child's discovery that she lacks a penis. Her lack inherently ('it *can* happen') threatens his deprivation. To this discovery Ferenczi and Freud[4] traced the petrifying, impotence-inducing image of Medusa's severed head. Beardsley, by means of a decorative elaboration that almost abolishes sex differences, makes of Salome a

[1]Quoted by Weintraub, *Beardsley*, VII: in a letter, with a drawing of the extracted tooth, Beardsley commented 'You see even my teeth are a little phallic.'

[2]*The Interpretation of Dreams*, VI (E), translated by A. A. Brill.

[3]'But the unconscious seems to contain nothing that would lend substance to the concept of the annihilation of life ... I am therefore inclined to adhere to the view that the fear of death should be regarded as analogous to the fear of castration.' (*Inhibitions, Symptoms and Anxiety*, VII, translated by Alix Strachey.)

[4]Freud, *Collected Papers*, Vol. II, XX.

AUBREY BEARDSLEY

Medusa petrified by the sight of her own head severed in a mirror. And it is significant that Beardsley *chose* to illustrate that tableau; it was the publication of that drawing which provoked the commission for the rest of the *Salome* pictures.

As his disease advanced, Beardsley increasingly transformed his ruling image of the Madonna into Venus, the heroine of his novel. It required the goddess of explicitly sexual love to cast a protective robe round a child increasingly terrified by castration fears. The Madonna's breasts were too chaste, too limited to the dispensing of spiritual Christian charity, to nourish a child increasingly greedy of life as he was progressively starved of it. At the end of his career, Beardsley solidified his rococo into baroque: first the Second-Empire baroque of his *Mademoiselle de Maupin* illustrations, and then the final, heavy-breasted baroque of his *Volpone*. Just as he made his rococo pictures emblematic of rococo elegance itself, he builds his great mounds of fruitful baroque ornamentation into a baroque metaphor of greed – at once Volpone's greed and Beardsley's greed for life. The drawings are bitter with Beardsley's sense of the futility of piling up baroque treasure on earth. Treasure, of which Beardsley, who died dunned, had so little, will avail neither him nor Volpone against death. Beardsley could not even be sure, and his contemporaries did not assure him, that by depicting these piles of objects he was building his own monumental tomb and immortality.

In the initial letters for his *Volpone*, 'M' (33) is still

mother; her son is still with her; it is still an altar, now a baroque one, that frames them. But she is now Venus, he Cupid, and both are paganly naked. A bitter sensual sadness surrounds them. The child's wings are bedraggled and he reaches towards his mother in desperation. Even Venus's breasts cannot satisfy this hunger. The extent of his hunger is clear from the caryatids that frame the altar. They are caprices fantasized from the many-breasted Ephesian Diana, capable of offering the child six breasts apiece. But of course their breasts are made of stone.

Beardsley's child's-eye-view is sometimes an embryo's-eye-view. Many of Beardsley's monsters represent himself. He surely did not depict Wagner's Alberich (34) as a sort of chinese gooseberry mixed with a sea-slug or write, in his novel, of 'the black, hateful sounds in Alberich's love-making' without taking thought that Alberich is a name cognate with Aubrey. The embryo or, as he described the one who acts as a page in the hat-shop in 'Choosing the New Hat', the 'unstrangled abortion',[1] is a motif which Beardsley compulsively employed: on small pretext, as when he illustrated Lucian[2] and Dante,[3] or none at all, as in his series of non-illustrative grotesques which, commissioned in 1893 to decorate three volumes of compiled *Bon-Mots*, allowed Beardsley to bring forth a free-association stream of Bosch-like fantasies and monstrosities. The persistent embryo may perhaps indeed have

[1] Quoted by Weintraub, *Beardsley*, VII.   [2] See Reade, *Beardsley*, plate 255.
[3] See Reade, *Beardsley*, plate 273.

ALBERICH

E

had one of the real-life occasions scholars have hypothe-sized; but essentially it is a self-portrait. Even the embryo in evening-dress (35), who very probably *is* Beardsley's friend and admirer Max Beerbohm, is also Beardsley. For Beerbohm, too, was precocious and precociously famous. It was his own precociousness Beardsley drew in embryonic form, together with his physical unviability. The essence of embryo is the vast head on the feeble, unfit-to-live body of a crustacean snatched from its shell; Beardsley is express-ing the consumptive poet's dread that his body's unfitness will make him cease to be before his pen has gleaned the teeming brain inside that huge foetal skull. One (36) of Beardsley's foetal vignettes, as revealing as a doodle, is macabrely explicit. Out of the top of the embryo rises a skeleton. It is Beardsley's autobiography in shorthand: from womb to tomb without having truly lived.

To speak of a Beardsley revival, whose beginning one would have to date somewhere about 1963 or '64, could easily be an exaggeration. Beardsley has been and to some extent still is slighted, but he has never in fact been for-gotten since the day, which was a fortnight after his death, that the *New York Times*[1] declared his work 'already ... well-nigh forgotten'. And probably the *New York Times* was simply telling a lie, in the way moralistic people seem to feel justified in doing when they can see no other hope of diverting public attention from something they dis-approve of.

[1] Quoted by Weintraub, *Beardsley*, Foreword.

In England much of Beardsley's work was reprinted
after the Second World War, though it was also sometimes remaindered. What happened in the 'sixties is that
Beardsley was wafted back to the centre of fashion, on
the zephyrs – indeed, the Zeffirelli – of the *art nouveau*
revival (this one a genuine revival of something previously
obscured and despised). Beardsley's polymorphous perversity is precisely the 'kinkiness' prized on the Swinging
London scene. His designs sell, in 1968, as greetings cards,
in the slot next the camp 'thirties stills of Dietrich and
Carole Lombard. Some Forte's restaurants (for instance,
the one in Leicester Square) have illuminated signs after
Beardsley's 'Garçons de Café' composition (37). Beardsley,
highest of high Catholic camp (his drawings were listed
by Susan Sontag in 1964 in the canon of camp), has been
carried shoulder-high, on the pretty, bacchanal rout of
current camp-followers, into his kingdom, the trans-
vestitely dandified realm of Carnaby Street.

The respectable pundits have now underlined the
Beardsley bang with their own boomings. Really, they
might have mentioned Beardsley's greatness a little sooner.
More to a serviceable point, the bang has been grounded
in firm, square scholarship. The 1966 Beardsley Exhibition
in London was an important assembly, underscored by the
bibliographical scholarship of Brian Reade's catalogue and,
in 1967, his Beardsley book. The Stanley Weintraub
biography of 1967 conscientiously assembles the facts.

For understanding, however, Beardsley is still infinitely
safer at the hands of the interior decorators. At least they

will not blot out his eroticism. They will not, as a scholar did in 1967, remark on 'the exclusion of erotic overtones' from Beardsley's title page (38) for his novel or describe the 'sixteenth-century German goblet' which is part of its furnishings as appearing 'just as a student might have drawn it in a museum'. The drawing is in fact so a-ripple with 'erotic overtones' that Venus's very left hand has fallen into mimickry of the male sexual organs. The goblet, like the one in the 'Mirror of Love' design, is a stylized account of the Diana of Ephesus fantasy which Beardsley later made explicit in the *Volpone* initial 'M'. The landscape in the background is that genital landscape where Beardsley's story takes place. With what other significance would Beardsley have caused that fountain to ejaculate so precisely in the centre of the avenue?

Beardsley is still, I sniff out, treated with a *grudged* admiration, and the cause, I surmise, is a still persisting snobbery about his medium. I have several times called his drawings 'pictures', because that is what they are; and his own reference to 'picture-making', in the project for the magazine from which, if only he could stay alive, he obviously didn't mean to exclude his own work, shews that he knew they were, too. But there is a half-formed idiom (almost as unjust as the colloquialism whereby 'artist' means exclusively 'visual artist') which restricts the meaning of 'picture' to one done in oils or, at the least, colours of some sort. The tyranny of the easel painting is less stringent now than it was in Beardsley's life-time,

when it was nimbused in the mystique of the painting-smock, top lighting and the vie de Bohême. But it still exists, and it imposes a snobbery against the medium of print.

It is often forgotten that there were in fact *two* printing revolutions: one when print was invented, and a second when, in the nineteenth century, it became cheap. Beardsley's almost exclusive medium was, in one sense, black-and-white and, in a further sense, print – and cheapish print. His work was intended, was literally de-signed, to be reproduced, in as many copies as the public would take, in magazines the size and price of not very posh books.

No one could call Beardsley cheap. He is perhaps the only artist of any kind practising in the 'nineties who was never sentimental. But the snobbery against his medium wrinkles its nose and dismisses him as superficial or 'minor'. I imagine that during the period when Beardsley was sign-ing his A.B. initials in a monogram borrowed from Dürer's A.D.,[1] he was putting himself under the patronage of one of the few Old Masters to have broken through the snobbery barrier and be acknowledged on the strength more of his black-and-white than of his easel pictures.

Beardsley's adoption of – or at least his virtual limitation to – black-and-white was an accident of his circumstances, but an accident whose content is cardinal to his artistic development and personality. He did not *mean* to cut

[1] As he did on, e.g. his very Germanic frontispiece to *Pastor Sang* (reproduced in Reade, *Beardsley*, plate 263).

72

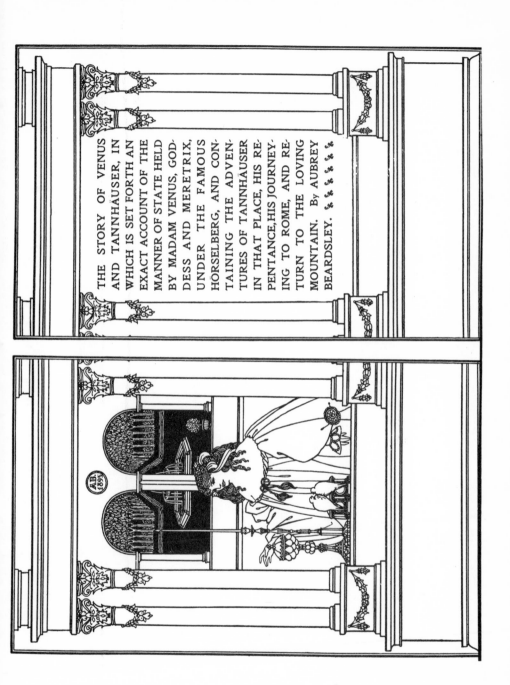

short his observance of the ritual apprenticeship at an art school. He did, occasionally, paint in oils. (And, of course, he designed posters as colour lithographs.[1]) What cut him off from conventional courses was the sheer lack of time, and presently lack of physical strength, imposed by his disease. And precisely *because* he lacked time Beardsley was driven to be modern.

Beardsley, who was admired by Toulouse-Lautrec[2] and, incidentally, Yvette Guilbert,[3] expressly upheld the poster – that is, large-scale printed work – as a modern form, arguing against the notion that a picture must be 'something told in oil or writ in water to be hung on a room's wall' and protesting against the 'general feeling that the artist who puts his art into the poster is *déclassé* – on the streets – and consequently of light character'.[4] But he was perhaps not even wholly aware of his own modernity in the matter of print at book-size. Unconsciously he solved the aesthetic crux on which picture-making was impaled, in the nineteenth century, by the invention of photography: without having to debate the point, he took pictures away from naturalism and towards decorative composition and image-making. By the same effortless stroke he solved the sociological problem. His work acknowledged that for modern people pictures are not things you hang on the walls of your country house and

[1]Cf., e.g., Reade, *Beardsley*, note 453.
[2]Cf. Weintraub, *Beardsley*, X.
[3]Cf. Weintraub, *Beardsley*, IX, note 6.
[4]Quoted by Weintraub, *Beardsley*, V, from Beardsley's article in the *New Review*.

absorb by leisured connoisseurship. They are things you look at reproduced in books. (Despite the pretensions of connoisseurship, the easel painting of the twentieth century, from Fauvism on, takes care to use its non-naturalistic flat colours in ways that will reproduce well.) Having worked all day, you look at the pictures in books by artificial light. The most modern thing of all about Beardsley was that he drew by the same type of light as his drawings would be seen by.

For Mr Reade, the 'morbid defect' of Beardsley's 'Ambassadors' drawing (30) in the 'Lysistrata' series is not 'the size of the phalluses' but 'the comic-cartoon rays which may symbolize an inflamed ulcer on the dwarf'. But Beardsley was drawing in the medium of the comic cartoon. It was a legitimate prong to his eclecticism that he should make occasional use of the idiom of the comic cartoon, as legitimate as Mozart's use of pop idiom when, during Figaro's aria 'Aprite un po' quegl'occhi', his orchestration calls in the horns to signify cuckoldry. In his frontispiece (39) to John Davidson's *Plays* (where Mabel Beardsley appears, naked, behind an Oscar Wilde whose legs are tied together), Beardsley caricatures the impresario Augustus Harris. It is in the pure language of *Comic Cuts* that he draws 'comic-cartoon rays' glittering off the presumably diamond stud in the centre of Harris's evening-dress shirt – and uses the stud to pin down the focal point of the complicated rhythm of light-sources and darkness in the design.

It was this exploitation of the graphic medium that made

Beardsley such a far-reaching pioneer. To the influences Beardsley is usually said to have exerted I would add one in, typically, a 'modern' medium developed out of the comic cartoon: it was Beardsley's disposition of white space which inspired the telling placing of Felix the Cat on a mainly white screen. And again: Beardsley, who drew John Bull (40) with a tiny erection under his enormous breeches[1] and redesigned the coinage of the realm by rendering Queen Victoria as a ballet dancer à la Degas (41), had gone a long way towards inventing the pop art use of jingoistic emblems. In his bitterness, he even invented, on a page of his sketchbook that Weintraub[2] quotes, the modern typographical joke. Beardsley wrote:

I

AM

TIRE

D

But black-and-white gave Beardsley far more than modernity. The violent, unmodified and unmodulated contrast of the two colours turned his medium itself into a metaphor of the ambivalence in his images and the tension in his designs. *Art nouveau* is a late, wintry, faintly deviant flowering of rococo, displaying the ultimate tendency of rococo design to fly apart from the centre, like

---

[1]Mr Reade (*Beardsley*, note 414) relates how a consortium including Bernard Shaw and George Moore obliged the publisher to – when it was too late to do so – withdraw the picture. However, Beardsley later did an expurgated version.
[2]*Beardsley*, VIII.

FIDEI DEFENSOR.

DEGAS

(41)

a firework or a rose at the very moment of disintegration. And even so, Beardsley's incredibly tensile design contrives to wire together the sparks or the petals even in the act of flying and falling. Even at the very end of his life, in the front cover for *Volpone* (42), he has exerted control over this Hammerklavier, whirligig, almost maddened-by-terror snowstorm of his fears of disintegration. And it is a black snowstorm: the last extension of the rococo stucco-work ceiling, turned funerary.

For black-and-white was in itself an image, for Beardsley, of the erosion of his life. In Beardsley, the medium is, to an exceptional extent, the image. Strictly, his medium is black *on* white. (His habit was to leave the white spaces in reserve. Only occasionally[1] did he scratch through his black to the white again or apply chinese white on top.) Black was encroaching on, eating into, the white space. Did he actually think of his lungs, in cockney or the language of offal-dealers, as his lights?

In 1894, when he took to using his black to create night scenes (43), he was trying to make death acceptable by eroticizing it. But his night scenes creep with his terror. By 1896 he confessed,[2] 'I am quite paralysed with fear.' And in the picture (26) of himself peering out from bed it is a black tent that is closing in to eclipse him, who is unavailed by even the term of a maternal satyr keeping watch.

His rococo compositions culminate in his lethal 'Barber' (6), whose mindless, inexorable face is the face of a clock,

[1] Cf. Reade, *Beardsley*, notes 363, 413.
[2] In a letter (quoted by Derek Stanford).

F

surmounted and surrounded by a hair-do coiled into the outline of a French gilt timepiece. The barber clipping the princess's hair – and cutting her life – is Time clipping Cupid's (and Beardsley's) wings. Time was Beardsley's executioner.

And likewise with the culmination of his baroque metaphors of greed. In the initial 'M' for the *Volpone* series, the hungry child is surrounded by breasts and cannot feed. In an initial 'S' (44), Beardsley confesses that he is destined not to consume but to be consumed. He has drawn the bird of death itself swooping on him, hungry to peck out not his liver but his lights. And in a last drag gesture of defiant inappropriateness, Beardsley draped the creature in one of his flying phallic chandelier-tassels and set a dowager's tiara of orient pearls on its horrid brow.

BRIEF CHRONOLOGY

The Family

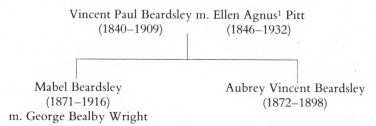

Vincent Paul Beardsley m. Ellen Agnus[1] Pitt
(1840–1909)   (1846–1932)

Mabel Beardsley   Aubrey Vincent Beardsley
(1871–1916)   (1872–1898)
m. George Bealby Wright

1870: Vincent and Ellen (Pitt) Beardsley married in Brighton (where both their children were born). The Pitts were a Brighton medical family. (A.B. claimed they were descended from the statesmen.) Vincent Beardsley, son of a jeweller of Clerkenwell, had capital of his own but quickly lost it (partly to settle a breach-of-promise action brought against him during his honeymoon).

1872: A.B. was born on August 21st at the house of his mother's father, Surgeon-Major William Pitt (of the Indian Army), 12 (now renumbered 31) Buckingham Road, Brighton.

During A.B.'s childhood, his father (who was tubercular) held several ill-paid jobs – with a telegraph company, and then with various brewers. Most of the family's small income (helped out by friends and by Surgeon-Major Pitt, who paid some of A.B.'s school fees) was earned by the mother, who gave French and piano lessons.

[1]It crosses my mind that this unusual second name may be a pun on the family name (see entry under 1884–5) Lamb. – B.B.

1878: A.B., who had already attended a kindergarten, went at the age of six as a boarder to Hamilton Lodge prep school in Sussex. In 1881 he moved, for his health's sake, to a prep school at Epsom.

1884–5: Mabel and Aubrey lived with their mother's aunt (according to Weintraub, Miss Lamb; according to the V. & A. exhibition catalogue, Miss Lambe) at 21 Lower Rock Gardens, Brighton. From here A.B. went to Brighton Grammar School as a day boy, becoming a boarder in January 1885.

1884–8: At Brighton, A.B. was at school with C. B. Cochran. His own interests, too, were largely theatrical. (A school play written by A.B. was produced in Brighton Pavilion by C. B. Cochran two years after A.B. had left the school.) A.B. was encouraged to act, write and draw by his housemaster, Arthur William King (1855–1922).

1888: In July, when he was still only fifteen, A.B. became a surveyor's clerk in London, where he lived with his family in Pimlico (at 32 Cambridge Street; then at 59 Charlwood Street; and then – from 1894 – at 114 Cambridge Street). Mabel and A.B. produced elaborate amateur theatrical performances at home.

1889: A.B. moved – still as a clerk – to an insurance office in Lombard Street. He was badly ill, with severe haemorrhages.

1890: A.B.'s first professional writing, an essay, was published in *Tit Bits*.

1891: On July 12th, Mabel and A.B. (aged eighteen) called at Sir Edward Burne-Jones's house in Fulham in the belief that his studio was open to the public. It wasn't. But B.-J. received them, looked at and praised A.B.'s drawings, and then gave the brother and sister tea on his lawn with his other guests, who included Mr and Mrs Oscar Wilde and their two children. The Wildes drove the Beardsleys back to Chelsea in their carriage afterwards.

autumn 1891–autumn 1892: While clerking by day, A.B. attended – on Burne-Jones's advice – evening classes under Fred Brown at the Westminster School of Art. A.B. left when Brown moved to the Slade.

1891–2: Through a Brighton friend, A.B. met Aymer Vallance, who presently introduced A.B. to William Morris (who didn't like A.B.'s drawings) and (on February 14th, 1892) to Robert Ross (who did and bought one).

(Vallance later compiled the 'iconography' to the Smithers *A Book of Fifty Drawings* by A.B. of 1897 and to the 1908 Ross study of A.B.).

In 1892, having inherited £500 from his Brighton great-aunt, A.B. made his first visit to Paris.

At home, he frequented the Jones and Evans bookshop, Queen Street, Cheapside, which was near the Guardian Life Assurance Company, where A.B. was a clerk. Frederick Evans introduced A.B. to J. M. Dent who, in the autumn of 1892, commissioned A.B., for £250, to design an edition of Malory's *Le Morte Darthur*. The more than 500 drawings took A.B. almost two years, and much pain, to complete. But on the strength of the commission, he gave up his job.

1893: the year A.B. became famous and twenty-one. In February, he began publishing drawings in the *Pall Mall Budget*. In April, the first number of the *Studio* appeared, with an article about A.B. by Joseph Pennell, illustrated by A.B. drawings, including some of the *Morte Darthur* pictures and 'J'ai baisé ta bouche Iokanaan', which A.B. had drawn to illustrate the original French version of Wilde's *Salome*, published in Paris early in 1893.

In May 1893, A.B. made his second visit to Paris, for the New Salon, where his personal elegance and fashionableness made a vast impression but angered J. M. Whistler (whose Peacock Room at 49 Princes' Gate A.B. had visited, admired and been influenced by in the summer of 1891). A.B. and Whistler thereafter feuded intermittently, by witticism and, on A.B.'s part, caricature (including one of Whistler's wife as 'The Fat Woman', a drawing John Lane refused to publish in the first *Yellow Book* for fear of Whistler).

In Paris A.B. went, with Pennell, to a performance of *Tristan*, after which A.B. did from memory his first design for 'The Wagnerites'.

A.B. received further commissions: from Lawrence and Bullen for thirty drawings for an edition of Lucian; from J. M. Dent for incidental grotesques to three volumes of compiled *Bon-Mots* (Charles Lamb and Douglas Jerrold, pub. 1893; Sydney Smith and Sheridan, pub. 1893; Samuel Foote and Theodore Hook, pub. 1894). Most importantly, the drawing for the French *Salome* led to a contract, in June 1893, from John Lane and Elkin Mathews, of the Bodley Head, Vigo Street, for A.B. to illustrate the English translation of the play with ten full-page drawings and a cover-design. (A.B. sold the copyright outright for fifty guineas.) A.B.'s original ambition was not to illustrate but to translate the text. (It was eventually translated by Lord Alfred Douglas.)

1894: the year of the *Yellow Book*.

In the new year Mabel and A.B. took a lease on 114 Cambridge Street. A.B. had some rooms decorated by Aymer

Vallance in orange and black. A.B.'s workroom was briefly shared by Will Rothenstein, who introduced A.B. to Max Beerbohm.

The Beardsley *Salome* appeared early in 1894.

A furore was created by A.B.'s poster for Shaw's *Arms and the Man* (produced by Florence Farr at the Avenue Theatre, near Charing Cross, in April 1894).

Also in April 1894 there appeared the first volume of the *Yellow Book*, a quarterly (conceived that new year) of which Henry Harland (1861–1905) was the literary and A.B. the art editor. (Harland and A.B., both consumptive, first met in their doctor's waiting-room.) The first two volumes were published by Lane and Mathews at the Bodley Head, the third and subsequent ones by Lane alone (Mathews having gone into independent business), still under the Bodley Head sign but from the other side of Vigo Street, at No. 8.

In July 1894, A.B. attended the unveiling of a bust to Keats in Hampstead church. Walter Sickert saw A.B. leave the ceremony through the churchyard and from memory painted his portrait of A.B. now in the Tate Gallery.

Volume III of the *Yellow Book* (October) contained two A.B. drawings published under the pseudonyms Philip Broughton and Albert Foschter. Reviewers ostentatiously preferred them to the work of A.B. After A.B. had disclosed his hoax, the 'Philip Broughton' was bought by Bernard Shaw.

1895: the year of the Wilde disaster.

After Volume V of the *Yellow Book*, due out in April, had been sent to press, Harland went to Paris and John Lane, accompanied by Richard le Gallienne, sailed to the United States. A.B. had intended to go with them and make an American lecture-tour but was too ill. Lane's assistant, Frederic Chapman, was in charge of the Bodley Head when

Wilde was arrested and accused of homosexual offences. Lane cabled home withdrawing Wilde's books from sale. At the time of his arrest Wilde was carrying a copy of Pierre Louÿs's *Aphrodite* bound, in the tradition of French novels, in yellow. The newspapers misreported it as a copy of the *Yellow Book*. Although Wilde had never contributed to the periodical (Lane had deliberately excluded him), a crowd mobbed Vigo Street and broke the Bodley Head windows. Although A.B.'s only collaboration with Wilde was the English *Salome* edition, several Bodley Head authors (including William Watson) threatened to withdraw their work unless Lane dismissed A.B. Mrs Humphry Ward also protested. As a result, Chapman, acting for Lane, withdrew all A.B. designs (except the spine and back cover, which were overlooked) from the April *Yellow Book*, which appeared a fortnight late, and A.B. lost his job and income as art editor. He and Mabel had to move from their house in Cambridge Street. It was in this year that Mabel Beardsley, after briefly teaching at the Polytechnic School for Girls, became a professional actress.

The scandal-value John Lane had thrown away in respectablizing the *Yellow Book* was quickly – in the second half of 1895 – picked up by Leonard Charles Smithers (1861–1907), Sheffield-born solicitor, London bookseller (with Henry Nichols, who in 1919 exhibited seventy fake Beardsleys in New York), scholar, publisher of erotica (and also, in 1897, when respectable publishers wouldn't have any truck with Wilde, of *The Ballad of Reading Gaol*), and presently (1899) bankrupt.

Smithers undertook to pay (but paid neither regularly nor in full) A.B. £25 a week for his exclusive services and started a new periodical, the *Savoy*, with A.B. as art editor and Arthur Symons (a *Yellow Book* contributor and flatmate of W. B. Yeats) as literary editor. The magazine's title was devised by A.B., who planned that Smithers should also publish, under another title, his not-yet-written novel, to which John Lane held the rights. In June 1895, A.B. took a three-year lease (surrendered in December) of 57 Chester Terrace but spent the summer and early autumn, very ill, in Dieppe and Paris, writing his novel and planning the *Savoy*. His design for the prospectus (later transferred to the inside cover) included a pierrot, to which Smithers objected on the grounds that it was too unserious for John Bull's taste. A.B. replaced it with a drawing of John Bull. It was George Moore who noticed A.B. had drawn an erection under John Bull's trousers. Moore and other intending *Savoy* contributors, including Shaw, persuaded Smithers to ask A.B. to alter the drawing. Smithers also made A.B. bowdlerize his original cover-design for the first volume of the *Savoy*, which shewed a cherub pissing on a copy of the *Yellow Book*.

1896: As a result of the alteration, the *Savoy* missed the Christmas 1895 market and the first number appeared in January 1896.

The second number (April) included fragments of A.B.'s novel and the first of his *Rape of the Lock* drawings (the series was for a Smithers edition).

In February, in unsuccessful search of health, A.B. went to Brussels, where he wrote his 'Barber' ballad (published in the *Savoy*) and where he was presently visited by the rich Russian-Jewish Catholic convert Marc André Raffalovich (1864–1934), friend of A.B.'s acquaintance (through Ada – the Sphinx – Leverson) John Gray, a poet who eventually became a Roman Catholic Canon in Edinburgh. It was for a volume of Raffalovich's that A.B. designed his 'Mirror of Love' frontispiece.

With its third number (July) the *Savoy* changed from a quarterly into a monthly. A.B. returned to London, was so ill that his doctor forbade him to work, and went to stay at Twyford, Sussex, then at an hotel in Epsom, where he did his *Lysistrata* drawings for a Smithers private edition, and then at Bournemouth. He arranged publication of past work (issued by Smithers as *A Book of Fifty Drawings*, 1897). The December issue of the *Savoy* was the last.

1897: Still too ill to return to London from Bournemouth, A.B., under the influence of Gray and Raffalovich, the latter of whom helped him financially, became a Catholic. In April he travelled to London for the last time, but only en route to France. He stayed at the Hotel Voltaire in Paris; in May he moved to St Germain, where he was disastrously ill; in July A.B. and his mother moved to the Hotel Sandwich, Dieppe, where he saw but didn't speak to Oscar Wilde. In September A.B. returned to Paris, and tried to raise money from Smithers by promising to complete his *Mademoiselle de Maupin* edition. In November he moved (having a haemorrhage at Dijon) to Mentone, to the Hôtel Cosmopolitan, where he worked on his *Volpone*, writing to Smithers that ''98 will either see my death or chef d'œuvres'.

1898: A.B. got out of bed and dressed to pose for a photograph (which Smithers published in 1899) sitting in a chair in his hotel room at Mentone, where Mantegna reproductions hang on the wall, A.B.'s candlesticks flank a crucifix on the bureau and a photograph of Raffalovich stands on the bookcase.

A.B. wrote, presumably to Smithers, a brief letter, which he signed with his name and 'In my death agony', asking for the destruction of '*all* copies of Lysistrata & bad drawings'.

He died in the presence of his mother and sister on March 16th.

Requiem Mass was celebrated in Mentone cathedral.

A.B.'s estate was valued on probate at £1,015 17s. 10d. (£836 17s. 10d. net).

Smithers published a *Volpone* edition with such of the

illustrations as A.B. had drawn (cover, frontispiece and five initial letters), with a eulogy of A.B. by Robert Ross.

1904: John Gray edited a collection of A.B.'s letters (mainly to Raffalovich) under the title *The Last Letters of Aubrey Beardsley*.

1908: A.B.'s mother was granted a small Civil List pension.

1916: Mabel (Beardsley) Bealby Wright died of cancer. In 1919 W. B. Yeats published his sequence 'Upon a Dying Lady', beginning: 'With the old kindness, the old distinguished grace,/She lies, her lovely piteous head amid dull red hair/ Propped upon pillows ... '

1932: A.B.'s mother died at Haywards Heath.

BIBLIOGRAPHY

Aubrey Beardsley, *Under The Hill,* completed by John Glassco (Olympia Press, 1966).

A Book of Fifty Drawings by Aubrey Beardsley, with an iconography by Aymer Vallance (Leonard Smithers, 1897).

A Second Book of Fifty Drawings by Aubrey Beardsley (Leonard Smithers, 1899).

Aubrey Beardsley Exhibition at the Victoria and Albert Museum 1966: catalogue by Brian Reade and Frank Dickinson.

Walter Crane, *William Morris to Whistler* (Bell, 1911).

Brian Reade, *Beardsley* (Studio Vista, 1967).

Robert Ross, *Aubrey Beardsley*, with iconography by Aymer Vallance (John Lane, The Bodley Head, 1908/9).

Susan Sontag, *Against Interpretation* (Farrar, Straus & Giroux, 1966).

Derek Stanford, ed., *Aubrey Beardsley's Erotic Universe* (Four Square, 1967).

R. A. Walker, ed., *The Best of Beardsley* (Spring Books, 1948).

Stanley Weintraub, *Beardsley. A Biography* (George Braziller, 1967).